The Secret to The Ravioli Recipes

Amazing New and Refined Ravioli Recipes

BY: Ivy Hope

IVY HOPE
COOKBOOK

Copyright/License Page

Table of Contents

Introduction

If you love eating Ravioli but haven't made it at home, because it is a lot of work and you didn't know-how, this cookbook is here to guide you how. This Ravioli cookbook has 30 amazing, unique, and easy to make Ravioli recipes that you can make at the comfort of your home with some common ingredients. From gourmet recipes to easy comfort meal recipes, this cookbook has it all. It is diverse in terms of its options and has a wide range of recipes.

It also has recipes that are a mix of two cuisines like the Ravioli stroganoff which is predominantly a Russian dish made from beef. Also, the wonton Ravioli is a mixture of Chinese and Italian cuisines mushed together to form one. Apart from this, the cookbook also consists of different variations of the dish like Ravioli casserole, Ravioli nachos, Ravioli Lasagna, Ravioli pizza, etc.

The dessert recipes are unique in this cookbook. Usually, Ravioli is a savory dish. But with a little experimentation, you can get some of the best Ravioli desserts that exist in the world. With a little imagination and skills, this cookbook presents you with some of the best dessert Ravioli recipes like- peaches and cream brown rice Ravioli, chocolate Ravioli filled with raspberry cream, s'mores Ravioli, etc.

So, with a little help from this cookbook, get ready to be a MasterChef in your own kitchen and cook up some of the best Ravioli dishes that exist.

Egg Ravioli

A very different idea as compared to the normal stuffed Ravioli, Egg Ravioli is one of the best appetizers. And when you cut it and take a bite, it melts in your mouth and leaves a delicious after-taste. The filling is so cheesy and leaves an unforgettable taste. So, let's get started so that you can treat yourselves with the goodness of this dish.

Ingredients:

- Ricotta cheese, fat-free- ½ cup
- Fresh basil, chopped- 2 and ½ teaspoon
- Extra virgin olive oil- 4 teaspoons
- Lemon rind, grated- 2 teaspoons
- Grounded black pepper- ½ teaspoon
- Kosher salt- ¼ teaspoon
- Parmesan cheese, grated- 1/12 cup
- Wonton wrappers- 16
- Unbroken egg yolks- 8
- Egg white, lightly beaten- 1
- Fresh chives, chopped- 4 teaspoons
- Lemon rind (for serving)- ¼ teaspoon

Serving Size: 8

Preparation time: 32 minutes

Instructions:

1. Take a bowl and add ricotta cheese, chopped fresh basil, olive oil, grated lemon rind, grounded black pepper, kosher salt, and Parmesan cheese. Mix everything nicely so that the flavors are evenly distributed.

2. Take the wonton wrappers and roll the wrappers with the help of rolling pin roll it out to 4 inches in diameter.

3. Now take a spoonful of the filling and place it in the middle of the wrapper. Now, using the back of a spoon, try making a well in the middle of the filling. The well should be around 1 and ½ inch in diameter and should be surrounded by the filling.

4. Now gently place a yolk on top without breaking it. This is the most crucial step. You have to be careful to not let the yolk break.

5. Now brush the edge of the wrapper with egg wash. This acts as the glue and helps to seal the edges. Press gently at the edges to seal properly.

6. Make sure that it doesn't open up while cooking. Do the same for the rest of the Raviolis.

7. Now take a pot and heat some water in it. Add some salt to this water. This will help the Ravioli to cook faster.

8. Now, carefully place the prepared Ravioli into them and let it cook for some time. It should take around 3 minutes for the Ravioli to get cooked.

9. The dough of the Ravioli should be cooked properly, and the yolk should be cooked but a little runny.

10. Once it is done, carefully take out the Ravioli from the pan and then place it on a plate. Sprinkle some lemon rind and chives on top of it before serving.

11. And voila! You have a delicious, mouthwatering appetizer to serve your guests. Enjoy!

Loaded Fried Ravioli Nachos

What is better than loaded nachos? Loaded fried Ravioli nachos! The perfect snack for a Saturday movie night or when you have your friends staying over! It is a very interesting substitution for the normal boring nacho chips. The jalapeno gives it a spicy flavor, and the best part is that they are quite easy to make and taste heavenly and delicious! So, let's get started with this mouthwatering snack!

Ingredients:

- Oil (for frying)- ½ cup
- Eggs- 2 large
- Mexican hot sauce- 1 tablespoon
- Water- 1 tablespoon
- Breadcrumbs- 1 and ½ cup
- Frozen cheese Ravioli- 40 pieces
- Grilled diced chicken- ½ cup
- Parmesan cheese, shredded- 1 and ½ cup
- Sour cream- ¼ cup
- Fresh lime juice- 1 tablespoon
- Pico de Gallo- 1 cup
- Fresh guacamole- ⅓ cup
- Cilantro leaves, chopped- ⅓ cup
- Black olives, sliced- 3 tablespoons
- Jalapeno slices- 5-6

Serving Size: 8

Preparation time: 40 minutes

Instructions:

1. For this recipe, we'll be needing a baking sheet. So first off, we should prepare the baking sheets. So, in the first rimmed baking sheet, we shall line it with aluminum foil. In the second baking sheet lined up with some paper towels, place a wire rack. Now, take a large pot and pour enough oil so that it makes a depth of 1 inch. Heat the oil.

2. Once the oil reaches a temperature of 325 °F we should fry the nachos. So, in the time when the oil is heating up, we shall prepare the Ravioli nachos. In a dish, take the eggs, some Mexican hot sauce, and water, and whisk it properly. Then in another shallow dish, take the breadcrumbs.

3. Now take the frozen cheese Ravioli and coat it nicely with the prepared egg-hot sauce mixture. Toss it and coat it properly before moving onto the dish with the breadcrumbs. Toss the Ravioli there so that the breadcrumbs stick properly to the Ravioli.

4. Now fry these Ravioli till they turn golden brown and become crispy. Using a slotted spoon, take out the Ravioli and transfer it to the wire rack to drain the excess oil.

5. Preheat the broiler with a rack. In the baking sheet lined with aluminum foil, arrange the Ravioli without much overlapping and top it with the grilled chicken and the grated cheese. Broil for about 2 mins until the cheese is bubbly.

6. In a bowl, whisk together lime juice and the sour cream nicely to make a sauce. Take out the baking sheet from the broiler and then top it off with some black olives, pico de gallo, cilantro, some pieces of jalapeno and guacamole. Drizzle some prepared lime cream on top and voila! You have a delicious plate of fried Ravioli nachos ready to chomp to while binging a show or hanging out with your friends.

Tomato Ravioli

Tomato Ravioli is a quick and easy to make meal. The tangy flavor of the tomato goes well with the cheesy Ravioli and the little heat of the black pepper. It is the perfect dinner for nights that you don't feel like putting a lot of effort in your dinner. It is healthy and easy to make! So, let's get started with the recipe!

Ingredients:

- Cherry tomatoes- 1 pound
- Onions, cut into wedges- 2
- Oil or cooking spray- ½ cup
- Olive oil- 3 tablespoons
- Balsamic vinegar- 2 tablespoons
- Kosher salt- ½ teaspoon
- Black pepper- ¼ teaspoon
- Cheese Ravioli- 20 pieces
- Fresh basil, chopped- 2 tablespoons

Serving Size: 4

Preparation time: 50 minutes

Instruction

1. Firstly, preheat the oven at 425 °F. Then, divide the tomatoes into two parts.

2. In one part, cut the tomatoes to halves and then arrange all these sliced as well as whole tomatoes along with the onions in a pan.

3. Make sure to coat the pan first with some cooking spray.

4. Add 1 tablespoon of olive oil to the mixture and let it bake for over 30 minutes at 425°F.

5. After 30-35 minutes, take out the pan and to it, add another 2 tablespoons of olive oil, balsamic vinegar, salt, and black pepper to it and then bake for another 10 minutes.

6. In the meanwhile, cook the readymade Ravioli in a pan of boiling water.

7. Take it out once it is cooked properly for about 3 minutes and reserve ¼ cup of the cooking water.

8. Mix the cooked Ravioli along with the tomatoes and mix them around properly. Add the cooking water and bake for another 5 minutes.

9. Serve hot with some chopped cilantro and you have yourself a very easy and healthy dinner ready!

Fried Ravioli

This is one of the easiest Ravioli recipes that exist! And so delicious that you can't have enough of it! It is the perfect snack to chomp away mindlessly. And all you need is a few ingredients, and the best thing about the recipe is that you don't really have to make the Ravioli. You can get a readymade Ravioli and improvise it to make a delicious snack!

Ingredients:

- Vegetable oil, for frying- ½ cup
- Large egg-1
- Milk- 2 tablespoons
- Seasoned breadcrumbs- ⅔ cup
- Refrigerated cheese Ravioli- 24
- Parmesan cheese, grated- ¼ cup
- Marinara sauce- 2 cups

Serving Size: 4

Preparation time: 15 minutes

Instructions

1. First off, in a wok take enough vegetable oil so that it is at least 1 inch deep. Heat the oil in medium flame and let the temperature get as high as 325°F.

2. Next, line a baking sheet with an aluminum foil and take a plate covered with absorbent paper.

3. Now, in another bowl, whisk together the egg and milk. Whisk properly to form a smooth mixture. In another shallow dish, take the seasoned breadcrumbs. Next, dip the Ravioli into the batter, remove the excess and then cover it with the seasoned breadcrumbs. Coat the Ravioli nicely and evenly with the breadcrumbs and then set it aside in the baking sheet. Do the same for the rest of the Ravioli.

4. Once the oil is hot enough, one by one, dip the Ravioli into the wok and let it fry for some time. Once it becomes golden brown in color, scoop it out with a slotted spoon and transfer it to the plate with the absorbing paper towel. This will soak the excess oil. Sprinkle some grated Parmesan cheese on top of the hot fried Ravioli.

5. In a pan, heat the marinara sauce for some time over medium-low heat. You can add some Mexican seasoning if you want. Scoop the sauce in a bowl and feel free to top it with some pico de gallo.

6. Serve these crispy, and tasty fried Ravioli with some hot marinara sauce!

Spinach Ravioli Lasagna

Another simple, healthy and pretty easy recipe to make is this spinach Ravioli lasagna. In this recipe, we switch up the normal lasagna recipe with our Ravioli lasagna. Instead of using lasagna noodles, we'll use Raviolis. It is just as tasty but with the goodness of some cheesy Ravioli. The cheesy alfredo sauce is mouthwatering! It is quite easy to make and a very good option for dinner. So, let's get started, shall we?

Ingredients:

- Fresh spinach leaves- 6 oz
- Pesto sauce- ⅓ cup
- Alfredo sauce- 15 oz
- Vegetable broth- ¼ cup
- Cheese Ravioli- 25 oz
- Italian cheese blend, shredded- 1 cup
- Basil (garnish)- ¼ teaspoon
- Paprika (garnish)- ½ teaspoon

Serving Size: 6

Preparation time: 35 minutes

Instructions

1. First things preheat the oven to 375°F. Next, wash the spinach leaves properly and chop them up. Take it in a bowl along with some pesto sauce and toss around nicely.

2. In another bowl, mix alfredo and vegetable broth and combine it nicely till it is smooth and mixed properly.

3. Take ⅓ of the alfredo sauce-vegetable broth mixture and then spread it in a lightly greased baking tray. Then, top it off with a layer of the spinach and pesto mixture. After that add half of the Cheese Ravioli on top of it.

4. Repeat again by spreading the alfredo sauce followed by the spinach leaves layer and finally another layer of the Cheese Ravioli.

5. Top the remaining alfredo sauce on top and put it in the oven to bake for 30 minutes.

6. After 30 minutes take it out from the oven and sprinkle the shredded cheese on top of it and then bake again for some time till the cheese melts. Garnish with some paprika and basil. Your spinach-Ravioli lasagna is ready to serve!

Ravioli Casserole

Ravioli casserole, the perfect comfort food. The recipe is so simple and it turns out amazing and very delicious. Secret tip? Just put loads of cheese in it!. The Ravioli is soft and tastes amazing along with the spaghetti sauce and the cheese. So, let's take a look at this recipe!

Ingredients:

- Frozen cheese Ravioli- 1 packet
- Cottage cheese- 2 cups
- Spaghetti sauce- 1 jar
- Mozzarella sauce- 4 cup
- Parmesan cheese- ¼ cup

Serving Size: 6

Preparation time: 60 minutes

Instructions

1. First of all, preheat the oven at 350°F. Take a baking dish and grease it properly with oil and then spread the sauce on the bottom. Layer half of the Ravioli on top of the sauce and then cover it with another layer of sauce. Top it off with some cottage cheese and 2 cups of mozzarella cheese.

2. Repeat the layers again with the remaining Ravioli and spaghetti sauce and finally top it off with some parmesan cheese.

3. Put the dish in the oven and let it bake for over 40 minutes till the cheese melts and becomes brown in color.

4. Take out after 40 minutes and let it cool down for a little bit before gorging on this cheesy deliciousness!

Toasted Ravioli

Toasted Ravioli, the perfect snack to munch on when you're bored. These are quite healthy and very easy to make. All you need is some store-bought cheese Ravioli, some Italian seasoned breadcrumbs, and a nice dip. These Ravioli are not fried but are toasted instead due to which they are crispier and healthier. So, no need of feeling guilty if you have too many of these!

Ingredients:

- Frozen cheese Ravioli- 24 pieces
- Seasoned Italian breadcrumbs- ½ cup
- Egg, beaten- 1
- Milk- ¼ cup
- Spaghetti sauce (to serve with)- 1 cup
- Parmesan cheese (for garnish)- ½ cup

Serving Size: 8

Preparation time: 30 minutes

Instructions

1. Firstly, preheat the oven at 425ºF. In a pot, take the salted water and boil it for some time. Add then add the frozen cheese Ravioli in it and let it cook for 2-3 minutes. After that, take it out of the pot and let it cool down to room temperature.

2. In a shallow dish, take some Italian seasoned breadcrumbs. In another dish take a beaten egg and add some milk to it. Whisk it together to form a mixture.

3. Now, take the boiled Ravioli and dip it in the egg mixture. Coat it nicely and let the excess drip out.

4. Transfer it to the dish with the breadcrumbs and coat it properly with it. Set it aside and continue the same for the rest of the Ravioli pieces.

5. Grease a baking tray and transfer the Ravioli in there and let it bake at 425ºF for 15- 20 minutes. Once its golden brown in color, take it out.

6. Serve hot with a bowl of spaghetti sauce and sprinkle some parmesan cheese on top of it.

3-bean Ravioli Minestrone

This is one of the easiest and fastest recipes to make. It is super healthy, delicious, easy to make and doesn't need many ingredients. This 3-bean Ravioli Minestrone is a lifesaver for a lazy day when you don't want to cook much but are feeling hungry. The soup is packed with the goodness of beans and has a delicious taste. It has a creamy consistency and makes you feel cozy on a cold rainy night! So, let's make this magical soup, shall we?

Ingredients:

- Onions, chopped- 1
- Celery, sliced- 2
- Carrots, chopped- 2
- Garlic cloves, minced- 2
- Chicken broth- 3 cans
- Baby lima beans, thawed- 9 oz
- Salt- ½ teaspoon
- Pepper- 1 teaspoon
- Italian seasoning- 2 teaspoons
- Diced tomato- 14 and ½ oz
- Garbanzo beans washed and drained- 16 oz
- Kidney beans rinsed and drained- 16 oz
- Olive oil- 1 tablespoon
- Parmesan cheese, shredded- ½ cup
- Mini cheese Ravioli- 7 oz

Serving Size: 14 cups

Preparation time: 40 minutes

Instructions

1. Take a large pot and add the chicken broth in it. To it add the onions, celery, carrots, garlic cloves, lima beans, diced tomatoes, kidney beans, and garbanzo beans. To it add the salt, pepper and the Italian seasoning.

2. And finally, drizzle some olive oil on top of it. Cover the pot and let it simmer for some 30 minutes.

3. After 30 minutes is over and the vegetables are soft and cooked nicely, add the cheese Ravioli in the pot and then let it cook for another 10 minutes.

4. Pour the soup in a bowl and serve with some shredded parmesan cheese. The result is so yummy and so healthy!

Cheese Ravioli with Pesto

This is a pretty easy recipe to make. Pesto and cheese can never go wrong! The pesto sauce gives the Ravioli a nutty flavor. The basil, spinach leaves, and garlic give the pesto an amazing aroma. The chicken broth makes the sauce yummier and helps the ravioli to be more flavorful. It is an easy recipe to make. So, let's start, shall we?

Ingredients:

- Fresh 3- cheese Ravioli- 1 packet
- Cherry tomatoes- 7-8
- Fresh baby spinach leaves- 1 ⅓ cups
- Fresh basil leaves- ⅔ cup
- Garlic cloves- 2
- Red pepper, crushed- ¼ teaspoon
- Salt- ½ teaspoon
- Olive oil- 2 tablespoons
- Fresh lemon juice- 1 tablespoon
- Pine nuts, toasted- ⅓ cup
- Chicken broth- 2 tablespoons
- Parmesan cheese, grated- ½ cup

Serving Size: 4

Preparation time: 12 minutes

Instructions

1. In a pot, boil some water and add the Ravioli to it and let it cook.

2. Meanwhile, in the food processor, add the spinach leaves, basil, garlic cloves, some salt, and red pepper. Let the food processor run and while it is running, add the lemon juice, chicken broth, and some olive oil. Let the food processor run until the mixture is smooth and creamy in texture.

3. Once the Ravioli is cooked properly, take it out of the pot. In a saucepan, heat some oil and add the cooked Ravioli, pesto and the cherry tomatoes in it. Mix everything properly so that the pesto sauce is evenly mixed with the Ravioli. Cook for around 2 minutes and then remove it from heat.

4. Serve this healthy and delicious plate with some grated parmesan cheese on top. Garnish with basil, if needed.

Bacon Pierogi Bake

Pierogi is a type of polish dumpling-like Ravioli which has a filling made from potatoes. So, here is a redefined recipe of a pierogi. Here, we make potato and onion Ravioli with a creamy sauce and top it with crispy bacon strips, tomatoes, and green onions. The crunch of the bacon is amazing against the soft filling of the ravioli. It is quite an easy recipe to make, so let's start with it.

Ingredients:

- Plum tomato, chopped- ¼ cup
- Green onions, sliced, - ¼ cup
- Garlic cloves- 2
- Black pepper, grounded- ½ teaspoon
- Cooking spray- 2 tablespoons
- cheddar cheese, grated- ½ cup
- Cream cheese (less fat)- ⅓ cup
- Chicken broth- ½ cup
- Bacon strips, chopped- 2
- Frozen potato and onion Ravioli- 1 packet

Serving Size: 4

Preparation time: 35 minutes

Instructions

1. First things first, preheat the oven to 400°F. Then in a skillet, add some oil and fry the chopped bacon strips in it until it is crispy. In the meanwhile, coat the baking tray by spraying it with cooking spray all over. Arrange the Ravioli in the baking tray.

2. Once the bacon is done, remove it and set it aside. In the same pan, add the chopped garlic pieces and stir for some time till it becomes golden brown in color. Then add the cream cheese to it and keep stirring it nicely until the cream cheese melts.

3. Once the cream cheese is melted properly, start adding the chicken broth to it, stirring continuously while doing so. Make sure that they mix properly to have a smooth texture. Let it simmer for some time till the consistency is thick enough. Then, pour the sauce over the Ravioli in the baking tray. Pour it evenly all over the tray so that it coats the Ravioli evenly.

4. Now, add the shredded cheddar cheese on top of it and let it bake for some 20 minutes. Once the cheese starts to melt and becomes a little brown in color, take it out of the oven. Top it off with some crispy bacon, onions, tomatoes, and pepper and serve hot!

Wonton Ravioli with Apple Cider Glaze

This wonton Ravioli has a Chinese twist to the traditional Ravioli recipes. And what can be better than a mix of Italian and Chinese cuisines! The Ravioli is stuffed with a delicious filling made from ground turkey, ground pork, and cheese. The apple cider glaze gives it a sweet and sour taste which juxtaposes the salty taste of the filling. This is something that you can make at home and will not want to miss out on. So, let's take a look at this recipe.

Ingredients:

For the Apple cider glaze:

- Apple cider- 4 cups
- Freshly ground black pepper- 1 and ½ teaspoon

For the Ravioli:

- Ground turkey-½ lbs.
- Ground beef-½ lbs.
- Onion- 1
- Garlic cloves, minced- 2
- Fresh sage, roughly chopped- 2
- Asiago cheese, finely grated- ½ cup
- Freshly ground pepper- 1 teaspoon
- Wonton wrappers- 60 round wrappers
- Egg, for egg wash- 1
- Chives, finely chopped- ½ cup
- Salt, to taste

Serving Size: 4

Preparation time: 60 minutes

Instructions

For Apple cider:

1. First, heat your pan to a high temperature. Then add the apple cider to it and let it boil.

2. Once the apple cider is reduced to half with a thick consistency, add a little grounded black pepper to it and then set it aside.

For Wonton:

1. First of all, in a pan boil some water with salt in it. Then reduce the flame to bring it to a gentle boil.

2. Next, to make the filling, in a bowl take ground turkey, ground beef, minced onions, minced garlic cloves, roughly chopped sage, Asiago cheese, ground pepper, and some salt to taste. Mix all the contents in the bowl thoroughly to incorporate.

3. To assemble the wonton Ravioli, take a round wonton wrapper and place it on a dry, clean surface. With a brush, coat the wrapper with egg wash thoroughly. While doing that cover the wonton wrapper so that the egg wash doesn't get dried up.

4. Put a spoonful of the filling in the middle of the wrapper. Cover this up by gently placing another wonton wrapper on top.

5. Be careful to place the corners carefully so that they overlap each other.

6. Gently seal the edges of the two wonton wrappers by pressing them gently. Now, lift the wonton gently, hands cupping over the filling region.

7. Press out any air inside and press around the rim to secure. Place it aside and do the same with the rest of the wontons.

8. To cook, place five wontons in the pan with boiling water and let it cook for some time. Halfway through the cooking process flip it to the other side and let it cook for some more time.

9. The meat inside is cooked when it is no longer pink in color. This should be done within 5-7 minutes. Make sure that the water is boiling.

10. To serve, place the wontons in a large bowl and drizzle some previously prepared apple cider glaze on top of it. To top it off, sprinkle some chopped chives on top. And here, your wonton Ravioli with apple cider glaze is hot and ready to be devoured.

Ricotta Ravioli and Browned Poppy Seed Butter with Asparagus

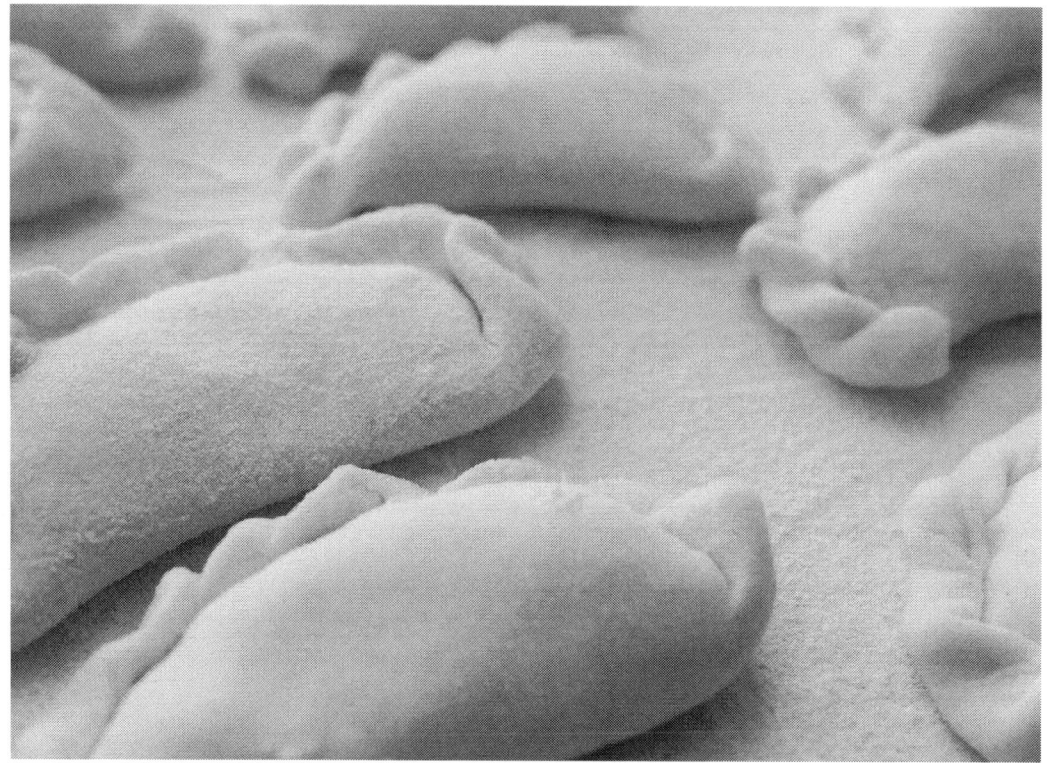

This mouthwatering dish is a pretty simple and healthy meal to make. The Ricotta Salata cheese used in this recipe gives it a sharp and slightly sweet flavor. You can also use Parmesan cheese instead of this cheese. The emerald asparagus against the black poppy seeds and the white Ravioli is strikingly beautiful. The recipe needs a little more work than usual, but it's worth all the work. So, let's dive into the recipe.

Ingredients:

For Ravioli:

- Ricotta cheese- 1 cup
- Pecorino cheese, grated- ¼ cup
- Flat-leaf parsley, minced- 2 tablespoons
- Salt- ⅛ teaspoon
- Egg white, large- 2
- Water- 5.6 liter
- Round gyoza wrappers- 48

For topping:

- Butter- 1 and ½ tablespoons
- Sliced asparagus- 2 cups
- Salt- ¼ teaspoon
- Poppy seeds- 2 teaspoons
- Ricotta Salata cheese- ⅓ cup

Serving Size: 6

Preparation time: 45 minutes

Instructions

1. Firstly, in a bowl take all the Ingredients needed for the filling- Ricotta cheese, Pecorino cheese, minced flat-leaf parsley, salt, egg-whites- and mix them properly with a fork so that it is blended nicely. This is our filling for the Ravioli.

2. Next, take a round gyoza wrapper and put two spoonfuls of the filling in the middle of the wrapper.

3. Then damp the corners of the wrapper with water and place another gyoza skin on top of it stretching lightly at the corners to meet the ends of the bottom wrapper.

4. Press the edges together with a fork to seal the edges.

5. Place these in a lightly floured baking pan and similarly make the rest of the Ravioli. Be sure to put a damp towel over it so that it doesn't dry up.

6. In a pan, boil the water over medium-high heat. Add 4-5 Ravioli at a time to cook. It takes 5 minutes to cook the Ravioli. Halfway through the cooking process, turn it to its other side and let it cook for some time.

7. After it is cooked properly, take it out and set it aside. Similarly, cook the rest of the Ravioli. After the Ravioli is cooked, reserve ½ cup of the cooking water. This water has all the flavor of the Ravioli and thus binds the flavors together.

8. Now, moving on to the topping. To make the topping, firstly heat a non-stick skillet and melt the butter over medium heat.

9. Stir it occasionally till the butter has melted completely and has started becoming light brown in color. To it, add asparagus, some salt and ¼ cup of the reserved cooking water.

10. Let the asparagus cook till the water is reduced completely. This will soften the asparagus and the cooking water will add some flavor to it.

11. Add some poppy seeds in it and stir it nicely for about 30 seconds, add the remaining ¼ cup of the cooking water and let it cook over medium heat for some time.

12. Once the water is reduced to about a half, add the already prepared Ravioli to the skillet and gently toss it around, mixing it with the topping.

13. Finally, add the Ricotta Salata cheese on top and serve immediately. Thus, your healthy and cheesy plate of Ricotta Ravioli and browned poppy seeds butter and asparagus is ready!

Pumpkin Ravioli with Sage Brown Butter

This is a fancier meal than the rest of the recipes. The sage brown butter melts in your mouth when you eat it. The flavors mix well together, and it tastes just as delicious as it looks. The sage gives a beautiful aroma to the ravioli. The lemon juice gives a little citrusy taste to the dish. The pumpkin gives it a sweet, creamy flavor in contrast to the sage brown butter which gives it a saltier edge. So, let's get started with this masterpiece!

Ingredients:

- Sage sprigs, divided- 2
- Butter- ½ cup
- Olive oil- 3 tablespoons
- Parmigiano- Reggiano cheese- ¾ cup
- Fresh lemon juice- 2 tablespoons
- Kosher salt- ½ teaspoon
- Wonton wrappers- 48
- Egg, lightly beaten-1 large

Serving Size: 1

Preparation time: 35 minutes

Instruction

1. Firstly, wash the sage sprigs. Then, take one of the sage sprigs and chop the leaves to get about 1 tablespoon of the chopped leaves.

2. Then, heat a skillet over medium heat. Add the butter to it along with a tablespoon of sage. Stir around continuously until the butter is lightly browned and fragrant. Stir continuously so that the butter doesn't burn. This should be done within 4-5 minutes.

3. Scoop out half of this mixture and keep it aside.

4. Now, to the skillet containing half of the sage, add the pumpkin puree, Parmigiano-Reggiano cheese, lemon, and salt and stir it continuously mixing it nicely.

5. The portion that was scooped out and kept aside should be mixed with two tablespoons of oil.

6. Take the wonton wrappers and brush the edges with some egg wash. This acts as a glue and will help to seal the Ravioli.

7. Take a spoonful of the filling prepared and place it in the middle of the wrapper. Take a second wonton wrapper and place it on top of the first one. Press the corners gently with your fingers and make sure that Ravioli is perfectly sealed.

8. In a large pot, bring some salted water to boil and one by one add the prepared Ravioli in it to cook. Cook till the Ravioli is tender and properly cooked. Once it is cooked properly, take it out from the pot with a slotted spoon and keep it aside.

9. For garnishing, take the second sage sprig to remove the leaves. Then take a skillet and heat one tablespoon of oil in medium heat. Add the removed sage leaves to the skillet and stir around till the leaves are crispy. Don't let it burn down. It should be done in 5-6 seconds.

10. Now, serve the prepared Ravioli with the prepared sage brown butter and garnish with some crispy sage leaves.

Giant Butternut Squash Ravioli

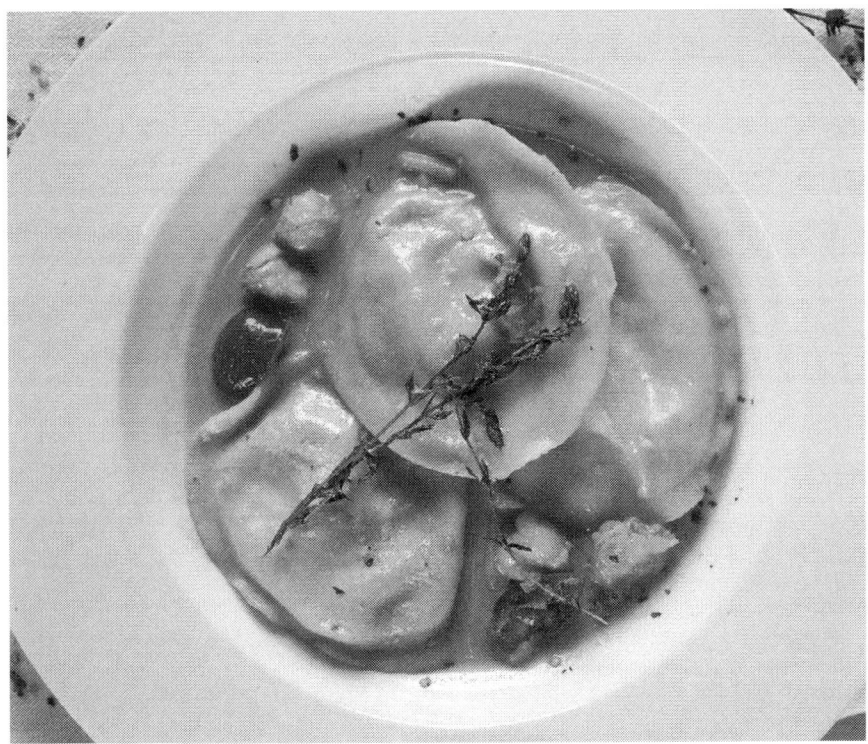

Why should we resort to small Ravioli pieces if we can make our own big ones? In this recipe, we will make giant butternut squash Ravioli. This is a longer recipe that needs a little more care and effort than usual. But once it's done, it's all worth it. The butternut has a creamy texture and tastes heavenly when paired with crunchy almonds, sage leaves, and some parmesan.

Ingredients:

For filling:

- Butternut squash, washed, peeled, seeds removed and cut into two- 1
- Salt to taste
- Grounded black pepper- 1 teaspoon
- Olive oil- 1 tablespoon
- Sage leaves, chopped- 1 tablespoon
- Toasted almonds- ¾ cup
- Nutmeg, freshly grated- ½ teaspoon
- Parmesan cheese, freshly grated- 1 ¾ cups

For assembling:

- Pasta sheets- 2
- Chicken broth- 1 Quart
- Fine semolina- 1 teaspoon
- Olive oil- 2 teaspoons
- Butter- 2 tablespoons
- Parmesan cheese, freshly grated- ½ cup
- Flat-leaf parsley, minced- 1 tablespoon

Serving Size: 8

Preparation time: 90 minutes

Instructions

1. First, we shall make the filling. Preheat the oven at 425°F. Then in a baking pan, take the chunky squash pieces and drizzle some olive oil on top of it. Then, season the squash with some salt and grounded black pepper.

2. Mix everything properly and let it bake for 45-50 minutes. In intervals of 15-20 minutes, stir the squash until they are very soft.

3. Scoop out this cooked squash from the baking tray and transfer it to the food processor. Be careful and do not burn your hand. Whirl it in the food processor until it is smooth and creamy in texture.

4. Scoop out the smooth squash paste from the food processor into a small bowl and let it cool down for some time. Add sage, nutmeg, almonds, and parmesan cheese to it and mix nicely.

5. Finally, add salt and pepper to taste. Your filling for the Ravioli is ready.

6. Now, we shall start assembling the Ravioli. Take a baking pan and line it with some parchment paper and sprinkle some semolina in it. Set it aside.

7. Now, in a clean board, lay out one of the pasta sheets. From one end, start putting two spoonfuls of the prepared filling on the sheet.

8. Maintain a 4-inch distance from the previous scoop and then put another scoop of the filling and so on. Around the edges covering the filling, brush some water there.

9. Next, slowly put another pasta sheet over the first one. Start from one side and place the pasta sheet carefully pressing around the filling. Be sure to not leave any air bubbles.

10. After the Ravioli is properly sealed, cut out any extra pasta dough. Transfer the Ravioli to the pan lined with the parchment paper.

11. In a large pot, boil some salted water and add one tablespoon of olive oil to it.

12. Add the prepared giant Ravioli to the salted water and let it cook for some time. This might take up to 5-7 minutes.

13. Check if the pasta dough has cooked properly. Once it's cooked properly, scoop it out with a slotted spoon and keep it aside.

14. In a pan, boil the chicken broth for some time. Once it is reduced to about one-third, add some butter to it.

15. Finally, to serve, take a giant butternut squash Ravioli in a soup plate. To it, add the prepared chicken broth and then finally garnish with some parsley and grated parmesan cheese.

One-pot Ravioli Pasta

A simple and quick recipe to make. It doesn't require much effort but tastes delicious and is considered a portion of good comfort food. We cook everything in one large pot combining all the flavors of the cooked beef that lingers in the sauce and it gives an amazing aroma. So, let's take a look!

Ingredients:

- Ground beef- 1 pound
- Mushroom, sliced- 1 packet
- Frozen cheese Ravioli- 24 pieces
- Mozzarella cheese, shredded- 1 cup
- Tomato-basil pasta sauce- 2 jars
- Onion, diced- 1
- Garlic cloves, minced- 2
- Salt- ½ teaspoon
- Pepper- ¼ teaspoon
- Water- 1 cup
- Dried Italian seasoning- 1 tablespoon
- Vegetable oil- 1 teaspoon

Serving Size: 4

Preparation time: 30 minutes

Instructions

1. Take a pot and heat some oil in it. Once the oil is hot enough, add the ground beef and cook for some time till the beef becomes light pink in color.

2. Once it is cooked properly, take it out and keep it aside.

3. In the same pot, sauté the onions and mushrooms till they become soft and the onion turns golden brown.

4. Add the garlic and sauté for a few seconds before adding in the cooked beef and tomato-basil pasta sauce.

5. Let it cook for some time before adding one cup of water to it.

6. Add some pepper, Italian seasoning and salt to the pot and mix everything nicely.

7. Cover the pot with a lid and let the contents inside simmer for some time.

8. Add the Ravioli after 3 minutes of letting it boil.

9. Cook for another 10-15 minutes till the Ravioli is soft and cooked properly.

10. Add the cheese after the Ravioli is cooked properly and serve immediately.

Ravioli Stroganoff

This recipe adds an Italian twist to the traditional Russian beef stroganoff. The sauce used in this recipe is cheesy and creamy. The mustard gives it a very strong and edgy flavor. This is a vegetarian version of the traditional beef stroganoff, but it tastes even better with the crispy and cheesy Ravioli pasta. The flavors are rich and strong and will keep you wanting more! So, let's get started with this delicious recipe!

Ingredients:

- Olive oil- 2 tablespoons
- Whipped cream cheese- 2 tablespoons
- Mushroom Ravioli- 16 pieces
- Mushroom gravy- 12-ounce jar
- Pearl onion, thawed and halved- 1 cup
- Mustard- 1 tablespoon
- Fresh parsley, chopped- ¼ cup
- Kosher salt- to taste
- Black pepper, crushed- ½ teaspoon

Serving Size: 4-6

Preparation time: 25 minutes

Instructions

1. In a pot, boil some water and add some salt to it. Once the water starts boiling, add the Ravioli pieces and then let it cook for 5-6 minutes. After it is cooked, take it out from the pot with a slotted spoon and keep it on a plate.

2. In another skillet, add some olive oil. Once the oil is hot enough, add the onions and some salt and black pepper to it and stir it nicely. Keep cooking the onions till they become a light golden brown in color.

3. Once the onions change color, add the whipped cream cheese and the mustard. To it, slowly start adding the mushroom gravy and mix the contents nicely. Cover with some lid and let the gravy simmer.

4. Occasionally, stir a little to ensure that the gravy doesn't stick to the skillet. If it becomes too thick, add some reserved pasta water to it. Once the sauce is creamy and has a nice texture, remove it from the heat.

5. Add some of the chopped parsley to the sauce and stir it. Add the sauce over the plate of cooked mushroom Ravioli and finally garnish with the remaining parsley. Voila! You have in front of yourself a delicious plate of vegetarian Ravioli stroganoff!

Supreme Ravioli Pizza

What sounds more Italian than Ravioli? Pizza. So, why don't we try and make a Ravioli pizza? Doesn't that sound amazing? Well, it tastes amazing too! In this recipe, we replace the usual pizza base with Ravioli pasta and then bake it. The bottom of the pasta is crispy, but the top is cheesy. Put anything you want as your topping. Here we'll be using sausages, hams, mushroom, and pepperoni as our toppings. Another tip: be generous with your pizza sauce and cheese because that is what makes a pizza taste the best, right? Now, let's get started with this recipe, shall we?

Ingredients:

- Large square Ravioli cheese- 48 pieces
- Olive oil- 3 tablespoons
- Crumbled Italian sausage, cooked- 1 cup
- Sliced pepperoni- ¾ cup
- White button mushroom- 8
- Sliced ham, chopped- 2
- Red bell pepper, diced- 1
- Onions, thinly sliced- ¼
- Fresh basil- 1 cup
- Eggs, beaten- 2
- Parmesan cheese, grated- 1 and ¾ cups
- Mozzarella, grated- 2 cups
- Pizza sauce- 1 and ½ cups
- Kosher salt- to taste

Serving Size: 6-8

Preparation time: 1 hour 10 minutes

Instructions

1. First of all, preheat the oven to 425°F. Next, in a pot, take some water, add salt to it and bring it to boil. Add the Ravioli in it and let it cook for some time till the dough gets soft.

2. Take a half- sheet pan and brush it nicely with olive oil so that the cheese doesn't stick to it. Then, to the base, add ½ cup of shredded parmesan cheese to it.

3. After 1-2 minutes, drain out the Ravioli and let it cool down for a little bit. Be careful not to cook the Ravioli all the way. Once the Ravioli has dried, transfer it to a bowl and to it add beaten eggs, ½ teaspoon salt, olive oil, and ½ cup grated parmesan cheese. Mix all the Ingredients properly.

4. Transfer the Ravioli to a baking tray and then bake for 25 minutes till it turns golden brown and cooks properly.

5. After 25 minutes, take it out of the oven and spread a generous amount of the pizza sauce on it. In the meanwhile, preheat the broiler.

6. Add the bell pepper, onions, mushrooms, ham, Italian sausage and pepperoni to it. Sprinkle the remaining parmesan cheese and mozzarella cheese on top of it.

7. Put it in the broiler till the cheese is melted properly and becomes a little brown in color. After 3 minutes, take it out. Serve with some basil leaves on top. Your homemade Ravioli pizza is ready to gorge upon!

Baked Spinach Ravioli

Delicious, cheesy, healthy, and easy to make Ravioli recipes! In this recipe, instead of frying the Ravioli, we boil it to maximize the flavors. Add in lots of spinach and any other greens if you wish. If you want to feed your kids some greens but are unable to do so, this is the perfect way to sneak some in. It tastes so delicious and creamy that they won't suspect any intrusion of greens in there!

Ingredients:

- Refrigerated cheese Ravioli- 20 pieces
- Garlic cloves, minced-2
- Small onion, chopped-1
- Fresh rosemary sprigs-2
- Spinach leaves, chopped-1 ¼ cups
- Whole milk- 2 cups
- Unsalted butter- 4 tablespoons
- All-purpose flour- ¼ cup
- Kosher salt- to taste
- Black pepper- ½ teaspoon
- Mozzarella cheese, cut into cubes- ¼ cup
- Parmesan cheese, grated- ¼ cup

Serving Size: 4

Preparation time: 30 minutes

Instructions

1. First of all, preheat the broiler. Then, take a skillet and melt the butter in it. To it, add onions, chopped garlic cloves, and rosemary and cook till the onion turns golden brown.

2. Then add the flour to the skillet and mix it nicely with the onions. Then, add 2 cups of water, milk, some salt, and black pepper.

3. Let it cook for some time and simmer for some more time. After some time, add the Ravioli to the sauce and let it cook for around 5 minutes. The Ravioli should cook properly and become soft. The sauce should also become creamy and should have a thicker consistency.

4. Once the Ravioli is cooked properly, take it off the heat and separate out the rosemary sprig and discard it. Add the chopped spinach leaves to the Ravioli and mix it up evenly.

5. Sprinkle some shredded parmesan and mozzarella cheese on top of it. You can be generous with the cheese if you want. Put this in the broiler and let it cook for over 5 minutes or until the cheese melts properly and becomes a little brown in color. Take it out once it is done and garnish with some Italian seasonings and serve hot!

Cheese Ravioli with Toasted Walnuts

This recipe of cheese Ravioli is so simple to make and has a rich flavor to it! The lemon juice used here, along with the toasted walnuts and flat-leafed parsley gives it a unique flavor and aroma. The tanginess of the lemon juice goes well with the cheesy flavor of the ravioli pasta. It is quick and easy to make and turns out delicious! The toasted walnuts give a beautiful aroma to the dish.

Ingredients:

- Cheese Ravioli- 24 pieces
- Walnuts- 1 cup
- Olive oil- ⅓ cup
- Lemon juice- 2 teaspoons
- Garlic cloves- 1
- Pepper- ½ teaspoon
- Kosher salt- to taste
- Flat-leafed parsley- ½ cup
- Parmesan, grated- ¼ cup

Serving Size: 4

Preparation time: 30 minutes

Instructions

1. Take a pot and heat some water in it. Add some salt in it and then add the cheese Ravioli to it. Let it cook for 5 minutes and take it out. Reserve 3 teaspoons of the cooking water.

2. Take a skillet and heat some oil in it. Add the garlic and walnuts and toss it around till the nuts are toasted and have some fragrance. Then add ½ teaspoon salt, ½ teaspoon black pepper, lemon juice, parsley and some of the reserved cooking water.

3. Then add the cooked Ravioli in the skillet and mix it around with the sauce. Serve it hot with some grated parmesan on top.

Chocolate Ravioli Filled with Raspberry Cream

This chocolate Ravioli recipe is a very unique idea for a dessert. The chocolate pasta dough and the rich and delicious raspberry cream are something to die for. The raspberry gives the filling a citrus-like flavor. The sweetness of the chocolate dough juxtaposes with the tartness of the raspberry filling. Make sure that the cream used as the filling is light and airy.

Ingredients:

- Flour- 2 ½ cups
- Cocoa- ⅓ cup
- Eggs- 3
- Water- ½ cup
- Sugar- 3 tablespoons
- Cream cheese- 10 oz
- Raspberry jam (pureed)- ½ cup
- Red food coloring (optional)- 3-4 drops
- Superfine sugar (to taste)

Serving Size: 2

Preparation time: 60 minutes

Instructions

1. First, take a bowl and add 2 ½ cups of flour, 1/3 cup of cocoa and 3 eggs. Whisk them together by using an electric whisk or a manual whisk. To it, slowly add water. All this while keep whisking it properly.

2. Make sure to have no lumps in it. Knead the dough properly with the right-hand movements and pressure till the dough is smooth and elastic. If you have a dough hook, beat it till the dough is perfect with the right texture.

3. Cover the dough with a plastic wrap and refrigerate it for about one hour.

4. Take the cream cheese in another clean bowl and whisk it with a hand whisk or an electric whisk until it is smooth and creamy.

5. Add the Jam, superfine sugar and ½ of the egg to it and keep whisking it until you get a silky, smooth texture.

6. After one hour, take out the dough that was kept away and divide it into four sections.

7. Take a rolling pin and aboard. Flour the dough properly and slowly roll out the dough by using the rolling pin. If you have a pasta machine, you can use that to roll out the dough. Do the same for the rest of the three parts.

8. Using a cookie cutter, curve out round shaped cut-outs of the dough and set aside.

9. Take one of the cut-outs and put a spoonful of the raspberry filling in the center. Around the edge of that cut-out wet it with some water and then immediately place another round cut-out on top of it to cover it completely.

10. Press around the edges carefully to seal the edges. Keep it aside and do the same for the rest of the dough.

11. In a bowl, take some water and 3 tablespoons of sugar. Add 5-6 pieces of the prepared Ravioli at a time and let it boil for 2 and ½ minutes. Then flip it to the other side and let it cook for another 1 minute or so before taking it out.

12. Voila! You have your Chocolate Ravioli filled with raspberry filling ready. Serve hot along with some strong coffee or drizzle some chocolate sauce on top of it.

Apple Cinnamon Ravioli

Apple cinnamon Ravioli is a quite easy dessert to make. It is simple and quick to make and tastes heavenly. Moreover, you don't need a lot of Ingredients. Most of these Ingredients are found in every household, so you don't have to go looking for them from shop to shop. You can fry it or cook it like usual. You can serve it with some ice-cream or just drizzle some honey on top of it along with some caramelized apples.

Ingredients:

- Apples- 4
- Honey- ¼ cup
- Cinnamon – 1 teaspoon
- Lemon rind- 1 teaspoon
- Vanilla extract- 1 teaspoon
- Wonton wrappers- 24

Serving Size: 4

Preparation time: 20 minutes

Instructions

1. First, cut the apple into cubes.

2. Then in a bowl, take the diced apples and add the other ingredients: 1 teaspoon of cinnamon powder, 1 teaspoon of vanilla extract, 1 teaspoon of lemon rind and ¼ cup of honey.

3. Mix all these Ingredients nicely so that it is flavourful and evenly seasoned. Set it aside for some time.

4. Now, to finally make the Ravioli, take a wonton wrapper and add a spoonful of the prepared filling in the middle of the wrapper.

5. Wet the edges of the wrapper with water and put another wrapper on top to cover it. The water acts as a glue and helps it to seal the ends.

6. Press gently around the edges to seal the Ravioli. If you wish, you can use square wonton wrappers or in fact make your own pasta dough and give it any shape you want! Set the Ravioli aside and make the others the same way.

7. To cook the Ravioli, you can either fry it or cook it the normal way by boiling it. For this recipe, we'll fry the Ravioli so that it is crispier.

8. So, take a wok and heat some oil in it on medium flame.

9. Once the oil is hot, add the Ravioli one at a time. Put 4-5 Ravioli at a time.

10. Let it cook for some time. Halfway through it, flip the Ravioli to the other side so that it cooks evenly on both sides. The Ravioli should have a beautiful golden-brown color once it's done.

11. Take it out and put it on an absorbent paper and let it soak the oil.

12. Your Apple cinnamon Ravioli is ready! Serve it hot with some vanilla ice-cream and voila! You have an amazing dessert! The flavor of the cinnamon melts in your mouth along with the honey and the apples.

Carrot Dessert Ravioli

This dessert Ravioli has an Indian twist to an otherwise Italian dish. The Ravioli is filled with Gajar ka Halwa which is a carrot-based Indian dessert made with grated carrots, sugar, milk, etc. It is the perfect Indian dessert to serve on any occasion. You can serve it with tea or just as a snack!

Ingredients:

- Carrots, grated- 6
- Sugar- ½ cup
- Ghee-2 tablespoon
- Milk- 1 ½ cups
- Ricotta- ½ cup
- Cashew-½ cup
- Sultana-½ teaspoon
- Cardamom pods- 6
- Wonton wrappers- 40
- Oil (to fry)--½ cup
- Water (or egg wash, to seal the wrappers)- ½ cup

Serving Size: 20

Preparation time: 90 minutes

Instructions

1. First, make the filling because it takes some time to get it done. Start by heating a non-stick pan on medium flame and add the ghee to it.

2. Then add the already grated carrots to it. Let the carrots cook for some time till they soften. Keep stirring it in intervals of about 20 minutes so that the carrot doesn't get burned or stick to the pan.

3. Once the carrot becomes softer, add the milk and Ricotta to it and stir it properly. Mix everything nicely in the pan and let it cook till the milk evaporates and the contents in the pan thicken.

4. Keep stirring and mixing well occasionally to avoid anything sticking on the pan. It should take around half an hour to let the milk evaporate completely.

5. Crush the cardamom pods to get some powder. Add the sugar (3 tablespoons) and the powdered cardamom into the pan and mix everything properly. Slowly, the sugar starts to dissolve and become like syrup.

6. Stir continuously at this point, mixing everything very well. When all liquid in the pan is evaporated, the halwa is done. You can top it off with some cashew and almonds and keep it aside to cool down.

7. Now, finally to make the Ravioli, take a wrapper and fill it with a spoonful of the Gajar ka Halwa. Wash the edge with some egg white or simply by water. This will work as glue and will help to stick the wrappers together.

8. Cover this wrapper with another wonton wrapper on top. Seal the edge nicely by pressing it nicely. Be careful to avoid any air gaps. Make sure it is sealed properly so that it doesn't open up when fried.

9. Take a wok and heat the oil in it. Once the oil is hot enough, start adding the prepared Ravioli in the wok and start frying. Keep the heat on medium to avoid it getting burnt. After frying on one side, flip the Ravioli to fry on the other side.

10. Cook both the sides equally till they become golden-brown in color. It shouldn't take more than 5 minutes. Take it out on an absorbent paper to soak the excess oil.

11. Your Carrot Dessert Ravioli is ready! Serve with some hot tea or drizzle some cream or powdered sugar on top of it for the extra taste. If you wish, you can also serve with some home-made honey-spiced sauce. Enjoy this Indian Ravioli dessert!

Chocolate Hazelnut Dessert Ravioli

Chocolate hazelnut Ravioli is the easiest dessert Ravioli you can make. It's delicious and has a chocolate and hazelnut filling inside. You can make the pasta dough yourself or you can buy wonton wrappers to make the Ravioli. In this recipe, we are going to make the pasta dough for the Ravioli instead of the wonton wrappers. You can serve it along with caramel sauce or chopped nuts. The Ravioli is soft in texture with a sweet filling. It is also very easy to make. Instead of a chocolate hazelnut filling, you can replace it with a peanut butter filling if you like! So, let's take a look at this recipe.

Ingredients:

- Flour- 1 cup
- Eggs- 2
- Chocolate hazelnut spread- ⅔ cup

Serving Size: 4

Preparation time: 50 minutes

Instructions

1. First, make the pasta dough. On a clean surface, take 1 cup of flour and make a mountain with it. At the tip, make a dent- like a well.

2. Crack the eggs in the well and then bring in the flour to well to mix well with the eggs. Mix properly to obtain a crumbly dough. Once it is mixed properly, keep kneading the dough properly.

3. Use the pressure of your palm to knead the dough. Keep kneading till you get a smooth ball.

4. Let the dough rest for some time. Keep it aside in a cool place for about 15 minutes. Take a rolling pin and board and flour it properly. Then, take the dough and roll it out as much as you can.

5. Do not make the dough too thin or else it may tear while cooking.

6. Using a cookie cutter, cut out the Ravioli. You can use a round or a square cutter to cut out the Ravioli. Now, take one such cut-out and add a spoonful of the chocolate-hazelnut spread in the middle of the cut-out.

7. Wet the edges of this cut-out with water or egg wash. This will help to act as glue and seal the edges. So, put another cut-out on top of this and press the edges to seal them completely. Set it aside and do the same with the rest of the Ravioli.

8. In a wok, heat some water and then add the Ravioli to it. Let it cook for some time. Halfway through it, flip the Ravioli to the other side and then let it cook for some more time.

9. When the Ravioli is cooked, it shall float to the top of the water. Take it out with a spoon and set it aside on a plate.

10. Serve it with some powdered sugar, chocolate sauce or caramel sauce! You can also throw in some nuts if you want!

Fried Nutella Ravioli

This dish is another super quick and easy dessert Ravioli recipe to make on any given day. Since dessert and love mix quite well, this can be a sweet romantic gesture towards your significant other. May it be a date night or Valentine's day, we improvised this simple recipe to make it a little different and romantic. Instead of the regular circular or square Ravioli shapes, we'll serve heart-shaped Ravioli. You can serve it with some powdered sugar and strawberries.

Ingredients:

- Wonton wrappers- 20
- Oil- ½ cup
- Powdered sugar- 1 tablespoon
- Nutella- ½ cup

Serving Size: 4

Preparation time: 30 minutes

Instructions

1. We will use heart-shaped Ravioli instead of the normal ones. In order to do that, we shall take a heart-shaped cookie cutter and make cut-outs in the shape of a heart in the wonton wrappers.

2. Take one such cut-out and add a spoonful of Nutella at the center of the cut-out. Then wet the edges with water and place another cut-out on top of it to cover it. Press the edges gently to seal the gap.

3. Keep it aside and do the same for the rest of the pieces. Now, in a pan, take some oil and heat it on medium flame.

4. Once the oil is hot enough, place the Ravioli in the pan and let it cook for some time.

5. You can place 4-5 Ravioli at a time to cook. After 2 minutes or so, flip the Ravioli to the other side and let it cook for another 2 minutes. This will ensure that the Ravioli cooks evenly and has a crispiness to it.

6. Once that is done, scoop it out of the pan and onto an absorbing paper so that it absorbs the excess oil. Serve it with some strawberry and sprinkle some powdered sugar on top of it. Enjoy!

Strawberry and Blueberry Ravioli

There are days when you crave a dessert but feel the guilt to take too much sugar in your diet. For those days of cravings, we have the perfect dessert, which is quite easy to make and is sugar-free too! So, it's a win-win situation. You can serve it with vanilla or blueberry ice cream. The best part about this recipe? The Ravioli is baked, so there's no deep-frying and the crispiness of the Ravioli is still achieved! So, let's do some baking, shall we?

Ingredients:

- Strawberry, chopped- 1 and ½ cup
- Blueberry, quartered- 1 cup
- Pie crust- 2
- Vanilla Greek yogurt- ¼ cup

Serving Size: 12

Preparation time: 30 minutes

Instruction

1. First off, chop the strawberries into small cubes. You need to chop enough strawberries to fill 1 & ½ cup. Next, chop the blueberries into four parts to fill one full cup.

2. Put these all into a bowl and add ¼ cup of Greek yogurt to it and mix it properly. No sugar is added. The sweetness of the dessert is achieved from the berries. Set this aside. This will be our filling for the Ravioli. In the meanwhile, preheat the oven to 325 degrees.

3. To make the Ravioli, take one pie roll and then open it up. Make 9 cuts in it. Take the other pie roll and do the same with it. Take two similar pieces that can overlap each other perfectly.

4. Take a spoonful of the filling and put it on top of the pie roll. Then take the other piece that overlaps perfectly over the existing pie crust.

5. Wet the edges with water or some egg wash and then seal them together by pinching them. Be careful that the contents of the Ravioli don't spill out.

6. Take a baking tray and place these Ravioli. Brush the Ravioli with some melted butter on the top and then let it bake in a pre-heated oven for over 10 minutes.

7. Once they are done, they get a beautiful golden-brown color.

8. Serve it with some vanilla or blueberry ice cream or sprinkle some powdered sugar on top of it.

S'mores Ravioli

Imagine a cold winter night. You're curled up on your sofa with your favorite cozy blanket and an episode of FRIENDS is on. You have a cup of hot chocolate and some s'mores. What could be more perfect? A cup of hot chocolate and s' mores Ravioli! The Ravioli is crispy and the marshmallows give a soft and sticky texture to it. Pair it with some strawberry sauce and you won't be able to stop yourself from munching on these.

Ingredients:

For the Ravioli:

- Hershey's milk chocolate bar, cut into squares- 2 bars
- Flat rectangular marshmallow- 12
- Egg- 1
- Graham crackers crumbs- 1 cup
- Water- 1 tablespoon
- Pillsbury refrigerated rolled out pie crust- 1
- For the strawberry topping:
- White sugar- ½ cup
- Vanilla essence- 1 teaspoon
- Fresh strawberries- 1 pint

Serving Size: 4

Preparation time: 25 minutes

Instructions

1. First of all, take the pie crust and roll it out on a clean surface. Divide the crust into 12 squares and cut it. In the meanwhile, preheat the oven to 425°F.

2. On each of the squares place a piece of the Hershey's chocolate and a piece of the flat marshmallow and sprinkle some graham cracker crumbs on top. Cover each piece with another square sheet of the pie crust.

3. Brush the sides with some egg wash and pinch the edges with your fingers gently to seal the edges of the Ravioli.

4. Line a baking sheet with some parchment paper and place the Ravioli there one by one. In another bowl, whip the egg and water together and brush the Ravioli with the egg wash nicely.

5. Put the baking sheet in the preheated oven and bake till it turns golden-brown or is slightly cooked. This shall take about 8 minutes.

6. In the meanwhile, start working on your strawberry sauce. Chop up the strawberries roughly. In a pan, add the chopped strawberries, white sugar and one teaspoon of vanilla essence and cook for some time. Stir occasionally till the berries become soft.

7. Once the juice from the berries start releasing and the berries become soft, start smashing them around with the help of a wooden ladle. This will help to make the juice faster. Keep stirring occasionally.

8. Once the sauce is thick enough with the right consistency, remove it from the heat. This should be done in around 15 minutes.

9. After that, take ⅔ of the prepared sauce and put it in the blender to get a puree. Now, mix this puree to the remaining ⅓ part of the sauce.

10. Once the s'mores Ravioli is ready, serve it hot with the homemade strawberry sauce. And voila! You're sorted for a cozy night in!

Berry Pie Ravioli

These berry pie Raviolis are a pocket full of joy! The filling is made up of delicious and juicy berries which are all too easy to devour! The Ravioli has crispy sides but a soft and juicy in the middle. When it is baked, the berries tend to release their juices due to which it becomes softer in the middle. So, try to drain your fruit as much as you can so that it doesn't become soggy. Serve with some mixed jam or whipped cream, any way you like it!

Ingredients:

- Frozen mixed berries- 1 bag
- Sugar- ¼ cup
- Vanilla extract- 1 teaspoon
- Parchment paper
- Brown sugar- ¼ cup
- Egg, beaten- 1
- Cornstarch- 2 tablespoon
- Pie crust- 2 boxes

Serving Size: 6

Preparation time: 60 minutes

Instructions

1. Take a baking sheet and line it up with parchment paper. Preheat the oven to 400°F.

2. Now, start making the filling. In a bowl, take the mixed berries, white sugar, brown sugar, vanilla essence, and some cornflour. Mix everything nicely so that there is a nice mixture of the filling. Set it aside for some time.

3. Then, take on the pie crust and roll it out with the help of a rolling pin, till it is smooth and plain. Divide it into 12 rectangular boxes and cut it out. Do the same with the other pie crust.

4. After that, take a spoonful of the filling and place it in the middle of the rectangular cut-outs. Brush the edges of each of the rectangles with egg wash.

5. Put the other rectangular pie cut-out on top of the first one. Carefully press the edges of the dough so that they seal. Be careful to not let it tear. Place all the prepared Ravioli in the baking tray. Brush the remaining egg wash on top of all the Ravioli and put it in the oven.

6. Let it bake till the Ravioli starts to become a little golden brown in color. After 25-30 minutes, take the Ravioli out. Let it cool for some time. Serve these delicious berry-filled Ravioli with some whipped cream or berry jam!

Fried Plum Ravioli with Mint Cream

This dessert is as homey as any comfort food and as posh as any restaurant dish. It is quite delicious with some rich flavors involved. The mint cream juxtaposes with the sweetness of the plum filling. The plum syrup used for garnishing gives a strong flavor to it. The Ravioli is crunchy on the outside but has a soft and sweet interior. This is the perfect dessert to serve your guests when they come over.

Ingredients:

- Chilled heavy cream- ½ cup
- Lemon juice- 2 teaspoons
- Fresh mint leaves- 10
- Plum reserves- ⅔ cup
- Black plum, finely chopped- ⅓ cup
- Confectioners' sugar- 1 ½ tablespoons
- Vegetable oil- 6 cups
- Wonton wrappers- 12

Serving Size: 4

Preparation time: 3 hours

Instructions

1. First of all, take the plum reserve and drain it through a coarse sieve to extract the juice leaving the solids behind.

2. Transfer this syrup to another bowl and add the chopped plums into it.

3. Mix everything nicely. This is your filling.

4. Now, for the Ravioli, take the wonton wrapper and put a spoonful of the filling in the middle of the wrapper.

5. Dampen the corners with some water. Now fold the wrapper in half in a diagonal way to form a triangular shape.

6. Now, for the mint cream, take some mint leaves and lemon juice in a mortar and pestle and crush properly.

7. Transfer this concoction to a larger bowl and add in the chilled heavy cream and confectioners' sugar and whisk vigorously till the cream is fluffy and light.

8. Now, take a pot and heat some oil in it on medium heat.

9. Once the oil is hot enough, put in the Ravioli and let it fry till it becomes golden brown. This will take around 1-2 minutes. Once it is done, take it out with a slotted spoon and soak the extra oil by putting it on an absorbent paper towel.

10. Serve this crispy, hot and delicious Ravioli along with some mint cream on the side. Drizzle some plum syrup for an extra rich flavor.

Peaches and Cream Brown Rice Ravioli

The recipe is full of flavor and tastes delicious. The Ravioli has a delicious peach filling with a hint of cinnamon. The taste of the filling is heavenly and has just the right amount of flavors- not too sweet, not too tart. The coconut cream topping is light and fluffy and tastes amazing when paired with the peach filling. So, let's get started with this recipe!

Ingredients:

For filling:

- Peaches, cut to cubes- 6
- Sea salt- ¼ teaspoon
- Olive oil- 1 tablespoon
- Cinnamon powder- ¼ teaspoon
- Honey- 2 tablespoons

For Ravioli:

- Egg yolk- 2
- Olive oil- 1 teaspoon
- Sea salt- ¼ teaspoon
- Brown rice flour- 1 cup
- Water- ¼ cup
- Mochiko (brown rice flour and potato starch)- ¼ cup

For the coconut cream topping:

- Coconut milk- 1 can
- Honey- 1 tablespoon
- Sea salt- ¼ teaspoon

Serving Size: 4

Preparation time: 70 minutes

Instructions

1. First, we'll start by making the filling. For that, take a skillet and heat some oil in it. Add the chopped peaches to it and stir around till it soft. add the cinnamon powder and a pinch of salt and keep stirring until it starts to become a little brown.

2. Add the sweetener and let it cook for about a minute. By this time, caramelization starts and the peaches become brown. Cover the skillet and reduce the heat. Let it simmer for some time.

3. Keep stirring occasionally to avoid it sticking to the bottom of the skillet. After 15 minutes, when the peaches are soft and ready, remove the filling from the heat and transfer to another bowl and set it aside to let it cool down for a bit.

4. Now, let's make the dough for the Ravioli. For this, add the brown rice flour, mochiko, and salt in a dry bowl. Mix them and then add the egg yolk and the olive oil to it.

5. With the help of a spatula, mix all the Ingredients together. Mix for 2 minutes till you get a crumbly texture.

6. Dump out this crumbly mixture to a clean worktop and add ½ cup of water to it. Knead properly by giving pressure from your palm and make a dough.

7. The dough shouldn't be too sticky. Add some more brown flour rice to it if it is too sticky. Keep kneading properly till you get the texture you want.

8. Once you're done, keep away the dough in a bowl and cover with a damp towel.

9. Now finally, make the cream. Take all the Ingredients in a bowl and mix everything properly with a whisk till you get a light and fluffy cream.

10. To make the Ravioli, dust the worktop with some flour and then roll out the dough with the help of a rolling pin. Take a cookie cutter and make cut-outs.

11. Try not to waste the dough and make as many cut-outs as you want.

12. Take one such cut-out and place a spoonful of the prepared peach filling in the middle of it. Dampen one side with some water and fold the cut-out into half to have a taco shape.

13. Seal the ends properly with your fingers. Keep it aside and do the same with all the other Ravioli.

14. Boil a pot of salted water and put the Ravioli in it. Let it cook for 2-3 minutes till the dough has softened and cooked properly. Take it out from the pot with a slotted spoon.

15. Serve it hot with some coconut cream topped with cinnamon powder and honey! Gorge on this plate of deliciousness!

Pineapple Ravioli with Coconut Ice Cream

Saving the best for the last. With the goodness of pineapple, passion fruit, and coconut milk, this recipe is as wholesome as it can get. The pineapple, lemon juice, and the apple juice together give a citrus-like flavor to the filling. The coconut ice cream is light and mellow. The pineapple filling is absolutely lip-smacking and delicious. So, let's take a look at the secret of this amazing dessert, shall we?

Ingredients:

- Coconut milk- 1 can
- Vanilla syrup- ¼ teaspoon
- Lime zest- 1 teaspoon
- Pineapple, sliced- 1
- Egg white (for brushing)- 1
- Vanilla bean, sliced- 1
- Sugar- 2 cups
- Apple juice- ⅓ teaspoon
- Lemon juice- 1 tablespoon
- Passion fruit- 2
- Wonton wrappers- 24
- Butter- 1 tablespoon

Serving Size: 4

Preparation time: 90 minutes

Instructions

1. First, we shall make the ice cream. Combine the coconut milk, lime zest and vanilla syrup to the ice cream maker and let it run.

2. For the filling, take a pan and melt some butter in it. Add the pineapple slices to it and sauté for some time.

3. Then add the sliced vanilla bean and sugar to it and sauté all of it. After one minute or so, add the apple juice and the lemon juice to it to deglaze and let it simmer for about 30 minutes.

4. Cut the passion fruit into half and squeeze the juice into the pan. Let it cook for another 5 minutes and then put it off the heat.

5. Take a wonton wrapper and put a slice of the pineapple in the middle of the wrapper. Wash the borders with some egg wash and then cover the wrapper with another similar wrapper. Press the edges lightly to seal it. Be careful to remove the air bubbles from inside.

6. In a pot, boil some water and cook the Ravioli in it for 2-3 minutes till the Ravioli becomes soft and cooks properly. Once it is cooked, take it out from the pot with a slotted spoon and keep it on a plate.

7. Serve it with some ice cream and the compote from the filling. Garnish with some mint and voila! You have a very fruity and delicious dessert ready in minutes!

Conclusion

So, there you have it!

30 amazing ravioli recipes to make at home. The secret's out! Who said making ravioli is not for beginners? Here, in this book, we have all different kinds of recipes for amateurs as well as experts. We also have recipes for different courses of a meal- appetizers, entree, main course, and desserts.

So, don't get lazy and try out all these 30 amazing recipes and impress your guests. Some of these recipes are not just yummy but also very healthy. And on top of that, we have some ravioli dessert recipes! If this doesn't make you feel like a MasterChef winner, I don't know what will!

So, don't waste any more time and treat yourself with these mouth-watering dishes. And don't forget to use your imagination and make something different!

About the Author

Ivy's mission is to share her recipes with the world. Even though she is not a professional cook she has always had that flair toward cooking. Her hands create magic. She can make even the simplest recipe tastes superb. Everyone who has tried her food has astounding their compliments was what made her think about writing recipes.

She wanted everyone to have a taste of her creations aside from close family and friends. So, deciding to write recipes was her winning decision. She isn't interested in popularity, but how many people have her recipes reached and touched people. Each recipe in her cookbooks is special and has a special meaning in her life. This means that each recipe is created with attention and love. Every ingredient carefully picked, every combination tried and tested.

Her mission started on her birthday about 9 years ago, when her guests couldn't stop prizing the food on the table. The next thing she did was organizing an event where chefs from restaurants were tasting her recipes. This event gave her the courage to start spreading her recipes.

She has written many cookbooks and she is still working on more. There is no end in the art of cooking; all you need is inspiration, love, and dedication.

Author's Afterthoughts

THANK YOU

I am thankful for downloading this book and taking the time to read it. I know that you have learned a lot and you had a great time reading it. Writing books is the best way to share the skills I have with your and the best tips too.

I know that there are many books and choosing my book is amazing. I am thankful that you stopped and took time to decide. You made a great decision and I am sure that you enjoyed it.

I will be even happier if you provide honest feedback about my book. Feedbacks helped by growing and they still do. They help me to choose better content and new ideas. So, maybe your feedback can trigger an idea for my next book.

Thank you again

Sincerely

Ivy Hope

Printed in Great Britain
by Amazon